Calendar Patches
for Pillows, Quilts, and Clothing
Nancy J. Smith & Lynda S. Milligan

We hope you enjoy making the projects in this book as much as we did. The patterns are very versatile and can be used for the projects shown as well as on tote bags, jumper bibs, photo albums, and many others.
Have fun and enjoy!

 ## Thank You

Special Thanks to Sharon Gunderson, owner of *The Blue Rabbit Ltd.* in Littleton, Colorado, for allowing us to photograph in her gift shop. Many traditional folk art accessories are available from *The Blue Rabbit Ltd.* by calling 303-843-9419. JHB International, Gay Bowles Sales, and Apple Creek provided us with buttons. Fairfield Processing provided us with pillow forms. Thank you to Mary Pat Pogue.

 ## Credits

Editing — Sharon Holmes
Electronic Illustration — Susan O'Brien, Sharon Holmes
Cover Design & Photo Styling — Susan O'Brien
Consulting — Jane Dumler
Photography — Brian Birlauf

✩✩✩✩✩ POSSIBILITIES ®

…Publishers of *DreamSpinners®* patterns, *I'll Teach Myself®* sewing products, and *Possibilities®* books…

Calendar Patches For Pillows, Quilts, & Clothing
©1996 Nancy J. Smith & Lynda S. Milligan

✻ Calendar Patch Pillows

Pillow size is 14″. For best results, choose a firm cotton or homespun for pillow cover.

Yardage & Supplies for One Pillow (44″ fabric)

pillow cover fabric	¾ yd.
applique patch &/or calendar patch fabric	⅜ yd.
accent square fabric	⅜ yd.
applique fabrics	scraps

freezer paper
fusible web
14″ firm pillow form
four ¾″ to 1″ buttons for pillow
four ½″ to 1″ buttons for patch
fine-point permanent marking pen
tracing paper

✻ Make the Pillow Cover

Use an accurate ¼″ seam allowance throughout.

1. Cut fabric 21½″ x 30½″.
2. Press 2″ hem to wrong side of one 30½″ side of fabric rectangle. Press 2″ to wrong side again, forming a hem of double thickness.
3. Open pressed hem. Fold pillow cover in half with right sides together, matching 21½″ sides. Stitch as illustrated with a ¼″ seam allowance. Turn right side out. Press.
4. Refold and pin pressed hem in place. Stitch hem close to fold.
5. Make four buttonholes in top side of hem placed 3″ apart (3″-6″-9″-12″). Stitch buttons into position under buttonholes.

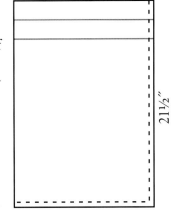

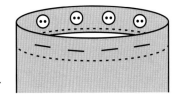

✻ Make the Applique Patch

1. Cut two 10½″ squares of applique patch fabric. Place squares right sides together.
2. Stitch around entire square, leaving about 2″ open on one side for turning. Clip corners, turn right side out, and press. Slipstitch opening closed.

✻ Fuse the Applique

1. Place rough side of fusible web against desired patterns. **Patterns are printed in reverse for easy tracing to fusible web.** Trace shapes on paper side, leaving a little space between shapes.
2. Cut shapes apart. Do not cut on the lines.
3. Place rough side of fusible web against wrong side of fabric. Bond according to manufacturer's directions.
4. Cut out shapes on the lines and gently peel off backing paper.
5. Using the photos as a guide, center fused applique pieces into position on applique patch.
6. Bond fused applique pieces to applique patch following manufacturer's directions.
7. If desired, machine applique pieces with an invisible zigzag stitch or a small machine blanket stitch.
8. Penstitch outlines of appliques and trace words with a fine-point permanent marking pen using a light box or a window with good light behind it.

✻ Make the Accent Square

1. Cut two 11½″ squares of accent fabric. Place squares right sides together.
2. Stitch around entire square, leaving about 2″ open on one side for turning. Clip corners, turn right side out, and press. Slipstitch opening closed.

✻ Assemble & Finish

1. Center appliqued square over accent square. Only about ¼″-½″ of the accent square will be showing. Pin together. Position patch on pressed pillow cover.
2. Attach patch to cover by stitching buttons at each corner through all layers. **OR:** Make buttonholes through applique patch and accent square at the same time. (See hint at top of page 3.) Position patch on pillow cover and mark button placement through buttonhole. Stitch buttons in place on pillow cover and button on patch. This allows you to use the same pillow cover with many different patches.

HINT: Make a template so that you can place buttons &/or buttonholes evenly. Place template at each corner of **applique patch** and mark at dot. Position buttons at marks and stitch.

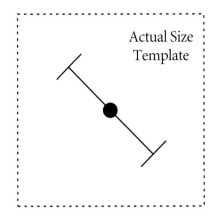

Actual Size
Template

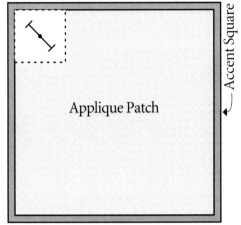

Applique Patch

Accent Square

✸ Make the Calendar Patch

1. Cut two 10½″ squares of calendar patch fabric.
2. Trace the calendar patch from page 4 on tracing paper.
3. Press 10½″ square of freezer paper to the wrong side of one fabric square (freezer paper stabilizes fabric and makes it easier to write on). Trace calendar from tracing paper to stabilized fabric with a fine-point permanent marking pen. Be sure to center calendar on fabric. To facilitate tracing, use a light table or a window with good light behind it.
4. Trace month name (at tops of pattern pages) and write in the dates. Trace desired icons from page 4 for special days (color in if desired), or make fusible appliques.
5. Place calendar patch pieces right sides together. Stitch patch pieces together, leaving about 2″ open on one side for turning. Turn and press.
6. Make accent square following *Make the Accent Square* directions on page 2.

NOTE: If making one applique patch pillow and one calendar patch pillow to display together, it looks nice to have the buttons on opposite ends of the pillow covers.

✸ Sweatshirt Topper

Yardage & Supplies (44″ fabric)

applique patch fabric	⅜ yd.
accent square fabric	⅜ yd.
applique fabrics	scraps
embroidery floss	1-2 skeins
fusible web	
fine-point permanent marking pen	
sweatshirt	

✸ Make & Attach the Patch

1. Carefully cut off ribbed waistband and cuffs from a purchased sweatshirt. Trim edges straight if necessary.
2. Fold approximately 1″ of the inside of the sweatshirt to the outside along bottom hem and cuffs.
3. Blanket stitch hems in place with 6 strands of embroidery floss.

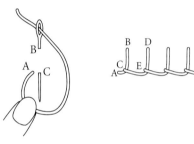

4. Fold ribbed neckband in half toward right side of sweatshirt. Blanket stitch in place.
5. Make applique patch: Cut two 9″ squares of applique patch fabric. Place right sides together. Stitch around entire square, leaving about 2″ open on one side for turning. Clip corners, turn right side out and press. Slipstitch opening closed.
6. Prepare and bond applique pieces following *Fuse the Applique* directions on page 2.
7. Prepare accent square following *Make the Accent Square* directions on page 2. Cut 10½″ squares instead of 11½″.
8. Center applique patch over accent square. Pin together. Blanket stitch applique patch to accent square with floss. About ¾″ of the accent square will be showing.
9. Place in position on center front of sweatshirt with patch about 1½″-2″ from neckline edge and centered from side to side. Blanket stitch to sweatshirt with floss.

Calendar Patch

   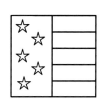 

Flag can be cut from preprinted fabric or from pattern.

MONTH
(dotted line is for placement only)

			+ Center of Block			

JANUARY

Snowman

Apply powder blush to snowman's cheeks with cotton swab. Use a fine-point, permanent marking pen for eyes, buttons, tree trunk, and snowflakes. We used Tulip Fine-line Paint Writer for calendar and snowflakes on pillows.

FEBRUARY

Angel

Apply powder blush to angel's cheeks with cotton swab. Use a fine-point, permanent marking pen for birdhouse poles, petals on daisy, and angel's face. For sweatshirt, cut applique patch 9˝ and accent square 10½˝.

MARCH

Mark sunflower petals and tulip stems with a fine-point permanent marking pen. Feel free to add more flowers and to design your own tools.

Apply powder blush to bunny's cheeks with cotton swab. Use a fine-point, permanent marking pen to mark facial features and to outline bunny legs.

Quilt can be set horizontally or vertically:
  54″ x 42″ (3 rows of 4 blocks for horizontal)
  42″ x 54″ (4 rows of 3 blocks for vertical)

Block Size   10″

Yardage (44″– 45″ fabric)

background	1 yd.
appliques	scraps
sashing squares	scraps to total 1 yd.
border	½ yd.
binding	½ yd.
backing	1¾ yds.

Additional Materials

fusible web	2 yds.
freezer paper	
fine-point permanent marking pen	

Cut

175 sashing squares (2½″)
12 background squares (10½″)
5 strips for border (2½″ x fabric width)
5 strips for binding (2½″ x fabric width)

Sew

1. Place rough side of fusible web against patterns. Trace shapes on paper side, leaving a little space between shapes. Group shapes that will be cut from the same fabric.
2. Cut shapes apart. Do not cut on the lines.
3. Place rough side of fusible web against wrong side of fabric. Bond according to manufacturer's directions.
4. Cut out shapes on the lines and gently peel off backing paper.
5. Bond appliques to centers of 10½″ background squares, using photos as a guide.
6. If desired, machine applique shapes to background squares. We used a small zigzag stitch and nylon thread so that stitches could not be seen.

7. If you wish to write on blocks, cut a piece of freezer paper about 10″ square and press to wrong side of block. Write with a permanent marking pen, testing first to make sure ink does not run. Use a light box or a sunlit window. Freezer paper can be used several times.

8. Sashing: Stitch five 2½″ squares into a row. Make 15 sets of five squares. Piece together 3 rows of 4 blocks and sashing, alternating sets of squares with blocks, referring to diagram and quilt photo. Stitch twenty-five 2½″ squares into a row. Make 4 rows. Piece rows together, alternating sets of twenty-five squares with rows of squares and appliqued blocks. Refer to photo.

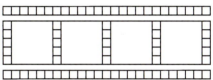

9. Press quilt top well.

10. Top & Bottom Borders: Measure width of quilt from cut edge to cut edge, placing tape measure across middle of one of the rows of blocks. Stitch border strips together end to end, if necessary. Cut top and bottom borders the measured length. Stitch to top and bottom of quilt. Press seams toward outside edge of quilt.

11. Side Borders: Measure length of quilt from cut edge to cut edge, as before. Stitch border strips together end to end, if necessary. Cut both side borders the measured length. Stitch to sides of quilt. Press seams toward outside edge of quilt.

12. Layer with backing and batting. Quilt as desired. We machine outline stitched the appliques and stitched each sashing square with an X. Bind with 2½″ strips folded lengthwise, wrong sides together.

13

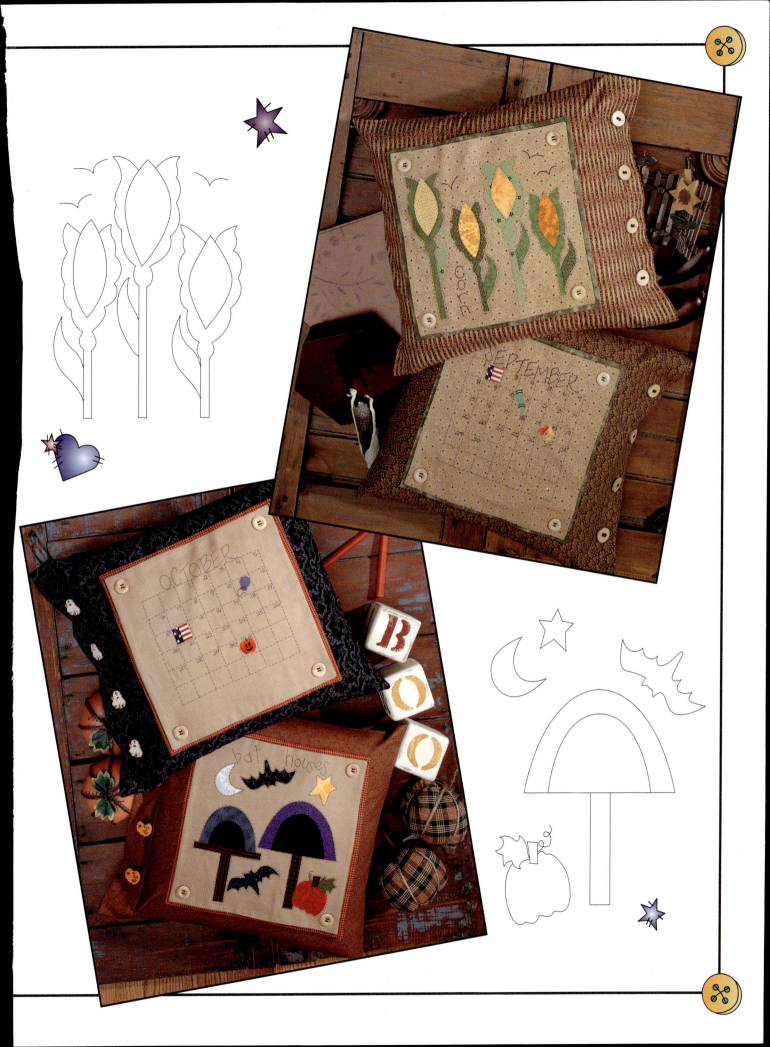

Mark sunflower petals with a fine-point permanent marking pen. Add more flowers if you like. Choose a fabric for the basket that looks woven.

JUNE

Note: Extend platform ½″.

birdhouses

Use buttons for birdhouse holes if desired. When tracing shapes, add ½″ to length of platform. Place the birdhouses about 1″ apart.

JULY

sunflower
star
Apple
flag

Cut a 3⅜″ x 4¼″ rectangle of white fabric. Cut blue square and red stripes and place on white background. Note that placement of applique pieces in quilt block and pillow are different.

19

AUGUST

Noah's fishing boat

We used a special Noah button and changed his position on the pillow. Use a permanent marking pen to mark facial features and fishing line. Use powder blush on a cotton swab to give Noah a healthy glow.

SEPTEMBER

corn

Use a fine-point permanent marking pen to mark birds. Place cornstalks a little further apart.

OCTOBER

bat houses

Use a fine-point permanent marking pen to make the pumpkin vine. Refer to photo when placing pieces.

NOVEMBER

If desired, change apples to miniature pumpkins for a pumpkin pie.
Look for fabrics with a textured feeling for piecrust.

DECEMBER

reindeer

happy

birthday

Make three reindeer (refer to photos). Use a fine-point permanent marker for eyes and powder blush applied with a cotton swab for cheeks. On the pillow and sweatshirt we used felt appliqued with a machine blanket stitch. For green pillow and sweatshirt, cut applique patch squares 9″ and accent squares 10½″. Birthday cake is a bonus pattern. Enlarge on a copier by 150%. Add as many candles as you like.